To: Jackie
Merry Christmas
2003!
Love, Sue, Keith, Mary and Gus

D0771025

Women & Cats

The History of a
Love Affair

It takes an essentially feminine and poetic nature to understand the cat.

Champfleury (Jules-Fleury Husson) (1821–82)
French writer

Published in 2003 by
Chicago Review Press, Incorporated
814 North Franklin Street
Chicago, Illinois 60610

ISBN 1-55652-513-3

Women and Cats – The History of a Love Affair by Michelle Lovric
Designed by Lisa Pentreath and Michelle Lovric
Conception and compilation copyright © 2002
Michelle Lovric, Covent Garden, London
Editorial Assistant: Kristina Blagojevitch
Printed in China by Imago

0 9 8 7 6 5 4 3 2 1

ACKNOWLEDGMENTS

Victorian chromolithographs from the archives of Mamelok Press
and the author's own collection.

"War Cat" by Dorothy Sayers, first published in *Time and Tide* in 1943 and
later in *The Poet's Cat*. Reprinted by courtesy of David Higham Associates Ltd.

Poems by Melissa Stein and Stephanie June Sorréll reprinted courtesy
of the authors.

Extract from *Carnevale* by M. R. Lovric, published by Virago Press.
Copyright © M. R. Lovric, 2001.

By associating with the cat, one only risks becoming richer.

Colette (1873–1954)
French novelist

Women & Cats

The History of a Love Affair

compiled by Michelle Lovric

CHICAGO
REVIEW
PRESS

Each night I read my cat
as she stalks me up the duvet
and pushes her head into my hands
Slowly, her deepening purr opens the
story of her day.
Between her whiskers, I find images of
leaf dance as she ecstatically claws tree bark.
Her ears prick, and I hear the scamper
of some winter famished shrew …
Enough!
The chapter is finished. Her teeth full stop my flesh.
She has jumped away;
for I cannot read what has not been invited, or written.
My cat will come again another night with
the next chapter for me to read like a book.

Stephanie June Sorréll (b. 1956)
English writer

Contents

Feline

... as a feminine her daintiness has led us to define her ...

George Robey
from *Jokes, Jibes and Jingles Jugged*, 1911

The Cat is a Princess of the Blood ... The Cat is always a Princess,
because everything nice in this world, everything fine, sensitive,
distinguished, everything beautiful, everything worth while, is of
essence Feminine, though it may be male by the accident of sex.

Letter to the editor of *The Yellow Book* from *The Yellow Dwarf*, Volume X, July 1896

For Puss is quite a lady in all her movements; and though she never
learned to dance, yet she walks with a step like a duchess ...

from *The Clan of the Cats*, 1877

Feminine

... of course, every cat is really the most beautiful woman in the room.

Edward Verrall Lucas (1868–1938)
English essayist and biographer

No Nautch dancer, no European Ballerina, has even approached her incomparable grace. While, as for her social virtues, who is there that knows them not? Her gentle urbanity, her sweet reasonableness, her suave dignity, her dainty curiosity and exquisite sense of cleanliness ...

Graham R. Tomson (Rosamund Ball Watson) (1863–1911)
English writer, from *Concerning Cats*, 1892

It is better, under certain circumstances, to be a cat than to be a duchess ... no duchess of the realm ever had more faithful retainers or half so abject subjects.

Helen M. Winslow (1851–1938)
American writer

Dear creature by the fire a-purr,
  Strange idol, eminently bland,
Miraculous puss! As o'er your fur
  I trail a negligible hand

And gaze into your gazing eyes,
  And wonder in a demi-dream
What mystery it is that lies
  Behind those slits that glare and gleam,

An exquisite enchantment falls
  About the portals of my sense;
Meandering through enormous halls
  I breathe luxurious frankincense.

An ampler air, a warmer June
  Enfold me, and my wondering eye
Salutes a more imperial moon
  Throned in a more resplendent sky

Than ever knew this northern shore.
  Oh, strange! For you are with me too,
And I, who am a cat once more,
  Follow the woman that was you …

Giles Lytton Strachey (1888–1932)
English writer

Next to a wife whom I idolise,
  give me a cat.

Mark Twain (1835–1910)
American writer

A fine lady is like a cat; when young, the
most gamesome and lively of all creatures
– when old, the most melancholy.

Alexander Pope (1688–1744)
English poet

I have found my love of cats
most helpful in understanding women.

John Simon

Granville, the author of "Les Animaux
peints par eux-mêmes", at the close of a
long series of observations recorded
seventy-five different expressions in a cat,
all more or less closely allied to the signs
of emotion or passion which constantly
diversify the human countenance.

Marius Vachon
19th-century French writer

Refined and delicate natures
understand the cat. Women, poets,
and artists hold it in great esteem …
only coarse natures fail to discern
the natural distinction of the animal.

Champfleury (Jules-Fleury Husson) (1821–82)
French writer

Is not the fair-haired beauty, as the ideal expression of grace, tenderness and kindness, the perennial feminine type sung by all poets, troubadours and minstrels, and painted by artists of all ages? And was not everything in the habits of the ladies and the lives they led perfectly adapted to the cat? ... and the cats themselves, crouching at their ladies' feet, must surely have purred rather than yelled, love songs full of fugitive subtleties, languishing melancholy, delicate and airy sentiment.

Marius Vachon
19th-century French writer

"Such a strange thing your liking cats, Mr. Gaunt," Ava said, as Pompey and Caesar took their seats on the two chairs at the side of the room where they could watch the table.
"They are very like women in their reactions – clever women."
"How?"
"They are uncontrollable – they only do what they please. They are timid and brave – selfish and indifferent, self-seeking, cupboard-loving – graceful, mysterious, vindictive – passionate and voluptuous. Sensuous always, sensual at moments. Contrary – and infinitely fascinating ..."

Elinor Glyn (1864–1943), English novelist,
a conversation between Ada Cleveland and John Gaunt
in her story "IT".

To nearly all women may fitly be applied the description of the "cat and the Fiddle". She is feline, not merely in the animal and the paltry sense of the word, but in the higher one which stamps the cat as the most sensitive, the most impressionable, the most loyal and the most intuitive of all creatures. A cat, like all beings, may be beguiled by touch, cajolings, dainties, but the cat of breed and life's experience is the most wonderful appreciator of character in Nature.

Mark Lane (b.1922)
from *The Eternal Feminine, A Little Book for Grown-up Men*

... when painters represented love, pleasure and luxury, and showed us scenes of domestic life and manners, the feline race reasserted its rights in artistic symbolism ... among the masters Cochin, Eisin, the Saint-Aubins, Gravelot, Debucourt, Moreau, Freudenberg, and others, whose drawings, engravings and etchings should be consulted ... to understand thorough the ways of Woman, with her airs, her charm, and her luxury, not one has failed to give the feline race an important position as illustrating the manners of the time, and on no account to be neglected by the artists if he would not be found guilty of defective taste and historical inaccuracy.

Marius Vachon
19th-century French writer

A French writer says, the three animals that waste
most time over their toilet are cats, flies, and women.

Charles H. Ross (1842(?)–97)
English writer

One of the characteristic instincts of the feline race
is a taste for elegance and dress ... when it is neither asleep
nor hunting game its one occupation is dressing itself ...

Marius Vachon
19th-century French writer

Nature has adorned her with a most beautiful coat, of the softest,
silkiest fur and loveliest of colours; and she spares no pains to
keep it clean and smart. I firmly believe that the cat is very proud
of her appearance, and likes to cut a dash – here again, by the bye,
she resembles the female of the human family ...

If you want to have your cat nice and clean, treat her now and
then to a square inch of fresh butter. It not only acts as a gentle
laxative, but, the grease, combining in her mouth with the
alkalinity of her saliva, forms a kind of natural cat-soap ...
If you wish to have a cat nicely done up for showing, touch her
all over with a sponge dipped in fresh cream, when she licks
herself the effect is wonderful.

William Gordon Stables (1840–1910)
Scottish writer, from *Cats: Their Points and Classification*, 1877

She is like the lady of fashion who so directs
her affairs that all necessary work shall be performed
by some one else and her own time left free for pleasure.
The cat gives the world nothing and receives from it
everything.

Georgina Stickland Gates (1896–1981)
American writer
from *The Modern Cat:*
Her Mind and Manners, 1928

A well-treated cat has a
great desire to look handsome and groomed.

Cora Sandel (Sara Fabricius) (1880–1974)
Norwegian writer
from "Two Cats in Paris and One in Florence"

She delighted in perfumes, stuck her little nose into bouquets, and
bit with little spasms of pleasure at handkerchiefs on which scent
had been put; she walked upon the dressing-table among the scent
bottles, smelling the stoppers, and if she had been allowed to do
so would no doubt have used powder. She was Séraphita, and
never did a cat bear a poetic name more worthily.

Théophile Gautier (1811–72)
French poet and writer

Men & Dogs

The men love their dogs;
the women, their cats.

Elizabeth Coatsworth (1893–1986)
American poet and writer

But – the Cat is subtle, the Cat is elusive, the Cat is not to be read at a glance, the Cat is not a simple equation. And so the Average Man, gross mutton-devouring, money-grubbing mechanism that he is, when he doesn't just torpidly tolerate her, distrusts her and dislikes her … the fatuous idgit never guesses how she scorns him.

Letter to the editor of *The Yellow Book* from *The Yellow Dwarf*, Volume X, July 1896

She … exhibits no such delight with the comfort of her surroundings as does the honest, unsophisticated dog.

George Robey
from *Jokes, Jibes and Jingles Jugged*, 1911

VS *Women & Cats*

Dogs I love, they carry their kridenshuls
in their faces, and kant hide them, but the
bulk ov cats reputashun lays buried in
their stumuk, az unkown tew themselves,
az tew enny boddy else.

Josh Billings (1818–85)
American humorist
from *Josh Billings, His Works Complete*, 1876

To Someone Very Good and Just,
Who has proved worthy of her trust,
A Cat will sometimes condescend –
The Dog is Everybody's Friend.

Oliver Herford (1863–1935)
English-born American humorist and writer

I prefer cats to dogs. They are more, far more independent, more natural. Human civilisation has not become a second nature to them. They are more primitive beings, more graceful than dogs; they take from society all that it can give them, and they always have a gutter to retire to in the vicinity of the salon where they may once more become what God has made them ...

Delphine de Sabran, Madame de Custine (1770–1826)
French writer

What makes me like cats so much better than dogs, is the way they have of looking straight and deep into one's eyes as if they would say something by their wondrous and mysterious glance.

Carmen Sylva (Queen Elizabeth of Rumania) (1843–1916)
Rumanian writer

The vanity of man revolts from the serene indifference of the cat.

Agnes Repplier (1858–1950)
American writer

The Cat's fastidiousness, her meticulous cleanliness, the time and the pains she bestows upon her toilet, and her almost morbid delicacy about certain more private errands, are among the material indications of her patrician nature. It were needless to allude to the vile habits and impudicity of the Dog.

Letter to the editor of *The Yellow Book* from *The Yellow Dwarf*, Volume X, July 1896

I remember at this moment, by-the-by, a curious companionship we had in those walks. A fine, big Newfoundland dog and small terrier were generally of the party; and, nothing daunted by their presence, an extremely tame and affectionate cat, who was a member of the family, invariably joined the procession, and would accompany us in our longest walks, trotting demurely along by herself, a little apart from the rest, though evidently considering herself a member of the party.

The dogs, fully occupied with each other, and with discursive raids right and left of the road, and parenthetical rushes in various directions for their own special delectation, would sometimes, returning to us at full gallop, tumble over poor puss and roll her unceremoniously down in their headlong career. She never, however, turned back for this, but, recovering her feet, with her back arched all but in two, and every hair of her tail standing on end with insulted dignity, vented in a series of spittings and swearings her opinion of dogs in general and those dogs in particular, and then resumed her own decently demure gait and deportment; thanking Heaven, I have no doubt, in her cat's soul, that she was not that disgustingly violent and ill-mannered beast – a dog.

Fanny Kemble (1809–93)
English actress

Special Relationships

According to Arab legend, the cat was born when Noah struck the lion violently on the nose: it sneezed and out came the first cat. This might seem to have parallels with Eve being extracted from Adam's rib ...

Hear and attend and listen; for this befell and behappened and became and was, O my Best Beloved, when the Tame animals were wild. The Dog was wild, and the Horse was wild, and the Cow was wild, and the Sheep was wild, and the Pig was wild – as wild as wild could be – and they walked in the Wet Wild Woods by their wild lones. But the wildest of all the wild animals was the Cat. He walked by himself, and all places were alike to him.

Of course the Man was wild too. He was dreadfully wild. He didn't even begin to be tame till he met the Woman, and she told him that she did not like living in his wild ways. She picked out a nice dry Cave, instead of a heap of wet leaves, to lie down in; and she strewed clean sand on the floor; and she lit a nice fire of wood at the back of the Cave; and she hung a dried wild-horse skin, tail-down, across the opening of the Cave; and she said, "Wipe your feet, dear, when you come in, and now we'll keep house." ...

Next day the Cat waited to see if any other Wild Thing would go up to the Cave, but no one moved in the Wet Wild Woods, so the Cat walked there by himself; and he saw the Woman milking the Cow, and he saw the light of the fire in the Cave, and he smelt the smell of the warm white milk.

Cat said, "O my Enemy and Wife of my Enemy, where did Wild Cow go?"

The Woman laughed and said, "Wild Thing out of the Wild Woods, go back to the Woods again, for I have braided up my hair, and I have put away the magic blade-bone, and we have no more need of either friends or servants in our Cave."

Cat said, "I am not a friend, and I am not a servant. I am the Cat who walks by himself, and I wish to come into your Cave." ...

Then the Woman laughed and said, "You are the Cat who walks by himself, and all places are alike to you. You are neither a friend nor a servant. You have said it yourself. Go away and walk by yourself in all places alike."

Then Cat pretended to be sorry and said, "Must I never come into the Cave? Must I never sit by the warm fire? Must I never drink the warm white milk? You are very wise and very beautiful. You should not be cruel even to a Cat."

Woman said, "I knew I was wise, but I did not know I was beautiful. So I will make a bargain with you. If ever I say one word in your praise, you may come into the Cave."

"And if you say two words in my praise?" said the Cat.

"I never shall," said the Woman, "but if I say two words in your praise, you may sit by the fire in the Cave."

"And if you say three words?" said the Cat.

"I never shall," said the Woman, "but if I say three words in your praise, you may drink the warm white milk three times a day for always and always and always."

Rudyard Kipling (1865–1936)
English writer
from "The Cat that Walked by Himself" in *Just So Stories*
(Of course, the Cat has His Way in the end, and extracts three compliments from the Woman.)

I was only a small child
when the seeds of cat enchantment
were sown within me.

May Eustace (b. 1904)
Cat breeder and writer

When we were children each of us had a cat.
It was grand when we gathered round the fire,
and the cats, in gala fur, beautifully clean and sleek,
sat majestically under their masters' chair.

Adèle (Athénaïs) Michelet (1826–99)
French writer

The neighbour's old cat often
Came to pay us a visit;
We made her a bow and curtsey,
Each with a compliment in it.

After her health we asked,
Our care and regard to evince –
(We have made the very same speeches
To many an old cat since).

Elizabeth Barrett Browning (1806–61)
English poet

The head favourite of my menagerie was a magnificent and very intelligent cat, "Ginger"… Ginger was as much the object of my idolatry as if she had had a temple and I had been a worshipper in ancient Egypt …

It was a good pious custom of my mother's to hear us our prayers every night … after which we were accustomed to recite a prayer of our affectionate suggestion, calling a blessing on the heads of all we knew and loved, which ran thus, "God bless papa, mamma, my dear sister, and Molly, and Betty, and Joe, and James, and all our good friends". One night, however, before my mother could pronounce her solemn "amen", a soft muttered "purr" issued from the cupboard, my heart echoed the appeal, and I added, "God bless Ginger the cat!" Wasn't my mother shocked! She shook both my shoulders and said, "What do you mean by that, you stupid child?" "May I not say 'Bless Ginger'?" I asked humbly. "Certainly not," said my mother emphatically. "Why, mamma?" "Because Ginger is not a Christian." "*Why* is not Ginger a Christian?" "Why? because Ginger is only an animal." "Am I a Christian, mamma, or an animal?" "I will not answer any more foolish questions to-night. Molly, take these children to bed, and do teach Sydney not to ask silly questions." So we were sent off in disgrace, but not before I had given Ginger a wink, whose bright eyes acknowledged the salute through the half-open door.

Lady Morgan (née Sydney Owenson) (1783–1859)
Irish writer

... this will be an incoherent letter because I have just been given a very engaging Persian kitten, named after St. Philip Neri (who was very sound on cats) and his opinion is that I have been given to *him*.

Evelyn Underhill (1875–1941)
English writer and mystic

22
...

They were at play, she and her cat,
And it was marvellous to mark
The white paw and the white hand pat
Each other in the deepening dark.

The stealthy little lady hid
Under her mittens' silken sheath
Her deadly agate nails that thrid
The silk-like dagger points of death.

The cat purred primly and drew in
Her claws that were of steel filed thin:
The devil was in it all the same.

And in the boudoir, while a shout
Of laughter in the air rang out,
Four sparks of phosphor shone like flame.

Paul Verlaine (1844–96)
French poet
translated by Arthur Symons

Deshoulières cares not for the smart
  Her bright eyes cause, disdainful hussy,
But, like a mouse, her idle heart
  Is captured by a Pussy.

Madame Deshoulières (1638–94), French poet,
referring to her cat, Grisette in a letter to her husband.

Madame Deshoulières was a favourite at the
Court of Louis XIV and also a great cat lover. She
wrote playful poems in the form of letters from
her cat, Grisette to the cats of some of her friends,
including the Duchesse de Béthune, whose cat was
named Dom Gris, and the Marquise de Montglas,
whose cat was called Tata.

What is the source of the love she bears me? ... She has the modesty that belongs to perfect lovers, and their dread of too insistent contacts. I shall not say much more about her. All the rest is silence, faithfulness, impacts of soul, the shadow of an azure shape on the blue paper that receives everything I write, the silent passage of paws silvered with moisture.

Colette (1873–1954)
French novelist

Bogey, love, Wingley is on my heart, awfully. I keep seeing him and remembering how he sat – a teapot cat – so serene in my room and how he touched my hand at meals with his gentle paw. You must love him tenderly – as you alone know how – and whisper him our secrets. No one else understands him. He's very like us, really.

Katherine Mansfield (1888–1923), New Zealand-born writer, from a letter to John Middleton Murry, September 24th, 1920.

Cat,
You are a strange creature.
You sit on your haunches
And yawn
But when you leap
I can almost hear the whine
of a released string,
And I look to see its flaccid shaking
In the place whence you sprang.

You carry your tail as a banner,
Slowly it passes my chair,
But when I look for you, you are on the table
Moving easily among the most delicate porcelains.
Your food is a matter of importance
And you are insistent on having
Your wants attended to,
And yet you will eat a bird and its feathers
Apparently without injury.

In the night, I hear you crying,
But if I try to find you
There are only the shadows of rhododendron leaves
Brushing the ground.
When you come in out of the rain,
All wet and with your tail full of burrs,
You fawn on me in coils and subtleties;
But once you are dry
You leave me with a gesture
of inconceivable impudence,
Conveyed by the vanishing quirk of your tail
As you slide through the open door.

Amy Lowell (1874–1925)
American poet, from "To Winky"

French writer Francis Augustus Moncrif relates an incident of a lady so dependent upon the nightly company of a cat that when she travelled she would sleep in the open rather than stay at an inn without a cat, or in a town where she might not borrow a cat for nocturnal company. She believed that without a cat she would be seized with severe illness.

Some years ago a suit was heard which made a great sensation. A brother demanded "interdiction" against his sister, because she "had had a tooth of her deceased cat set in a ring". This according to her brother, constituted a veritable act of madness and imbecility.

Champfleury (Jules-Fleury Husson) (1821–82)
French writer

In the 18th century Madame de Mirepoix
proudly exhibited to her friends some Angora cats
which she had taught to play lotto.

Marius Vachon
19th-century French writer

But see where mournful Puss, advancing, stood
With outstretched tail, cast looks of anxious woe
On melting Lizzy, in whose eye the tear
Stood tremulous; and thus would fain have said
If nature had not tied her struggling tongue:
"Unkind, O, who shall now with fattening milk,
With flesh, with bread, with fish beloved, and meat
Regale my taste? And at the cheerful fire,
Ah, who shall bask me in their downy lap?
Who shall invite me to the bed, and throw
The bed-clothes o'er me in the winter night?
When Eurus roars? Beneath whose soothing hand
Soft shall I purr? But now, when Lizzy's gone,
What is the dull, officious world to me?
I loathe the thoughts of life!" Thus plain'd the cat ...

James Thomson (1700–48)
Scottish poet
The poet wrote this poem for his sister, Elizabeth, recording her sorrowful
parting from her beloved cat on the day she had to go away to school.

Once a Goddess...

Pussy was a goddess in old Egypt,
and she has never forgotten it.
Old incense perfumes her soft fur.
A goddess in exile, she exacts honour
as any queen who has lost a realm
but will have her court and its courtiers.

Oswald Barron (1868–1939)
English writer and antiquary

She is connected with royalty ... and she therefore
appropriately leads a luxurious life, having a proper
aristocratic indifference to every thing which does not
minister to her own pleasure.

Thomas Brown
from *Interesting Anecdotes of the Animal Kingdom*, 1834

... cats dislike and despise us all. They take no trouble to
conceal it. No woman is a heroine to her own tabby. No
woman, it may be hazarded, is quite at her ease when writing
a love letter under the eye of her cat. They have been known
to turn the animal out of the room till the letter is finished.

Clennell Wilkinson (1883–1936)
English writer

The Cat is a victim of misunderstanding; who has never been really appreciated since Bubastis flourished; who has never taken her proper place in society ... this the cat resents.
A cat's resentment assumes two forms. The first of these is subtly insulting; and consists of scrupulously cleaning, with the tongue, any part of her glossy person that an objectionable hand has caressed. The second is more broadly offensive – more truculent; and consists in spitting.

George Robey
from *Jokes, Jibes and Jingles Jugged*, 1911

A cat's got her own opinion of human beings.
She don't say much, but you can tell enough
to make you anxious not to hear the whole of it.

Jerome K. Jerome (1859–1927)
English novelist and playwright

As between you and her, it is you who must do the toadying ... You must respect her pleasure. It is her pleasure to slumber, and do you disturb her: note the disdainful melancholy with which she silently comments your rudeness. It is her pleasure to be grave: tempt her to frolic, you will tempt in vain. It is her pleasure to be cold: nothing in human possibility can win a caress from her. It is her pleasure to be rid of your presence: only the physical influence of a closed door will persuade her to remain in the room with you.

Letter to the editor of *The Yellow Book*
from *The Yellow Dwarf*, Volume X, July 1896

Cats are like women and women like cats – they are both very ungrateful.

Damon Runyon (1884–1946)
American journalist and writer

When my cat and I entertain each other with mutual apish tricks, as playing with a garter, who knows but that I make my cat more sport than she makes me? Shall I conclude her to be simple? ... Nay, who knows but that it is a defect of my not understanding her language (for doubtless cats can talk and reason with one another) that we agree no better: and who knows but that she pities me for being no wiser than to play with her, and laughs and censures my folly for making sport of her when we two play together.

Michel Eyquem de Montaigne (1533–92)
French essayist

Women and cats will do as they please and

*N*obody ever tells me to do anything;
if they do I don't do it.

James Anthony Froude (1818–94)
English historian and man of letters
The she-cat's comment from *The Cat's Pilgrimage*, 1870

Cecilia is my woman. We are married.
I could purr and fawn around her to
reassure her about this, but I know a better
way to keep her love and attention. I treat
her coolly and this keeps her passionate,
and this keeps us both happy.

I don't often look her in the face when
she talks to me. Sometimes it is just too
much effort to mew so I open my mouth
silently to show that it has occurred to
me to address her. Cecilia understands.
We are married ... I would love her
more if we were not married, but that is
my nature.

M. R. Lovric (b. 1959)
British writer
from *Carnevale*

men and dogs should relax and get used to the idea.

Robert A. Heinlein (1907–88)
American science fiction writer

Most Fastidious Creatures

The domestic heart is her proper orbit;
comfort and kindliness her legitimate atmosphere.

Graham R. Tomson (Rosamund Ball Watson) (1863–1911)
English writer
from *Concerning Cats*, 1892

S... she accepts what is offered to her, only under protest as it were. She looks, smells, touches it with her paw; then, she gains confidence; if she takes the thing set before her it is that she considers it her due since it is offered; and if she likes it she makes it understood by her gracious air that she will be happy to accept some more.

Alexandre Dumas (1802–70)
French writer

He can recognise a cheap label with his eyes closed ...

Ann M. Foggatt
Contemporary English writer

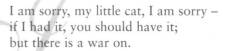

WAR CAT

I am sorry, my little cat, I am sorry –
if I had it, you should have it;
but there is a war on.

No, there are no table-scraps;
there was only an omelette
made from dehydrated eggs,
and baked apples to follow, and we finished it all.
The butcher has no lights,
the fishmonger has no cod's heads –
there is nothing for you
but cat-biscuit
and those remnants of yesterday's ham;
you must do your best with it.

Round and pathetic eyes,
baby mouth opened in a reproachful cry,
how can I explain to you?
I know, I know:
"Mistress, it is not nice;
the ham is very salt
and the cat-biscuit very dull,
I sniffed at it, and the smell was not enticing.
Do you not love me any more?
Mistress, I do my best for the war-effort;
I killed four mice last week,
yesterday I caught a young stoat.
You stroked and praised me,
you called me a clever cat.
What have I done to offend you?
I am industrious, I earn my keep;
I am not like the parrot, who sits there
using bad language and devouring
parrot-seed at eight-and-sixpence a pound
without working for it.

There is no justice;
if you have ceased to love me
there is no charity.

"See, now, I rub myself against your legs
to express my devotion,
which is not altered by any unkindness.
My little heart is contracted
because your goodwill is withdrawn from me;
my ribs are rubbing together
for lack of food,
but indeed I cannot eat this –
my soul revolts at the sight of it.
I have tried, believe me,
but it was like ashes in my mouth.
If your favour is departed
and your bowels of compassion are shut up,
then all that is left me
is to sit in a draught on the stone floor
and look miserable
till I die of starvation
and a broken heart."

Cat with the innocent face,
what can I say?
Everything is very hard on everybody.
If you were a little Greek cat,
or a little Polish cat,
there would be nothing for you at all,
not even cat-food:
indeed, you would be lucky
if you were not eaten yourself.
Think if you were a little Russian cat
prowling among the cinders of a deserted city!

Dorothy L. Sayers (1893–1957)
English writer

35
...

Last winter I had a visit of a week or two from my youngest niece, of nine years old. Wishing to have some small jollification before she went home, I thought it would be nice to have a pussies' tea-party, and as the prospect delighted her, we set to work to talk it over in earnest …

Next day, early in the afternoon, we prepared the feast. The invited guests were four grown pussies and two kittens, so we got ready four large and two small saucers. First a thick strip of fish was laid right across each saucer; an equal strip of cold rice pudding met it transversely, forming a cross-shaped figure that left four spaces in the angles. Thick cream was poured into these spaces, and the solid portion was decorated with tiny balls of butter, one rather larger in the middle, and two smaller on each of the rays. A reserve of fish and cream was to be at hand to replenish the portions most quickly exhausted …

At last the hour came, and meanwhile the excitement had grown intense. Five grown-ups were present, all as keenly interested as the little girl. The pussies were brought and placed on their stools, and the kittens, Chloe and Brindle, were put up to their saucers upon the table. To our great delight they all took in the situation at once … and they all set to work as if they were quite accustomed to tea-parties and knew that nice behaviour was expected …

Pinkieboy, as became the oldest and heaviest, finished his first, and after licking his saucer quite clean, and then his own lips, he looked round and clearly said, "That was very good, and please I should like a little more, especially fish and cream."

Gertrude Jekyll (1843–1932)
English garden designer and writer
from *Home and Garden*, 1900

Scratching, Spitting

Are cats revengeful? Never as a rule.
Yet they do sometimes display little pettish
outbursts of temper. They would not be like women
if they did not do that.

William Gordon Stables (1840–1910)
Scottish writer
from *Cats, Their Points and Classification*, 1877

I know some dames not less quarrelsome:
there is the wife of Henri des Argans,
who scratches and sets her back up like a cat.

Adam de la Halle (c. 1235–87)
French poet and composer
from *Jeu de Feuillée*

Yesterday was the fourth time Lenin visited since his arrival ... Poor Mimi
is making "Kuru" sounds. She impressed Lenin, who said that he had
seen such a magnificent animal only in Siberia and called her a majestic
cat. She even flirted with him, rolled on her back, and lured him to her.
When he attempted to approach her, however, she hit him with her little
paw and hissed like a tiger.

Rosa Luxemburg (1871–1919), German left-wing revolutionary,
from a letter to Kostia Zetkin, April 2nd, 1911.

&Sulking

Thou sidelong veerst with rump in air
Erected stiff, and gait awry,
Like madam in her tantrums high ...

Joanna Baillie (1762–1851)
Scottish playwright and poet

Gaze
With those bright languid segments green, and prick
Those velvet ears – but pr'ythee do not stick
Thy latent talons in me ...

John Keats (1793–1821)
English poet

Drat the cat.
And while I'm at it,
drat a few other people's cats as well.

Alice Thomas Ellis (b. 1932)
Welsh writer

That cat! I wish she were dead! But I can't shorten her days, because, you see, my poor, dear wee dog liked her. Well, there she is! And as long as she attends to Mr C. at his meals (and she doesn't care a sheaf of tobacco for him at any other time), so long will Mr C. continue to give her bits of meat and driblets of milk, to the ruination of the carpets and hearthrugs! I have over and over again pointed out to him the stains she has made, but he won't believe them her doings ... So what I wish is that you would shut up the poor creature when Mr C. has breakfast, dinner or tea; and if he remarks on her absence, say it was my express wish.

Jane Welsh Carlyle (1801–66)
Scottish woman of letters, wife of historian Thomas Carlyle

A feud between Gloria Swanson and Pola Negri,
Hollywood actresses

Gloria loved cats; Pola hated them. Pola ordered all cats banished from the lot. Her cohorts ran around the studio snatching up cats and dispatching them in bags. Gloria's loyalists scoured back alleys, rounding up stray cats to let loose inside the studio. Cans of milk were put out to woo there, titbits of liver thrown hither and yon.

In the still of the night Gloria's cats would be seized and cast out. In the morning two more would appear to take the place of every one. It couldn't continue indefinitely; even in Hollywood there's a limit on cats.

Hedda Hopper (1890–1966)
American journalist
from *Under My Hat*

French playwright Madame Girardin is said to owe to one of these furred aristocrats the failure of her play "Judith". A cat, outraged by the unpoetical rhodomontade of this ill-composed piece, rushed like a whirlwind on to the stage and began to mew like one demented. The whole audience burst into Homeric laughter; the curtain fell to rise no more on "Judith".

Marius Vachon
19th-century French writer

Stealth

Mostly, the cat loves
corners. What's peeking
round a doorframe,
dangling through a crack:
always the just-out-of-reach
sends him scrambling
on the strength of
his thighs. How
are we different, loving
what darts away – all feather
and tail – turning from
what we see fully, and recognize,
and could catch and keep?

Melissa Stein (b. 1969)
American poet

In time business becomes her pleasure ...

from *The Clan of the Cats*, 1877

Cats do not keep the mice away;
it is my belief that they preserve them
for the chase.

Oswald Barron (1868–1939)
English author and antiquary

&Subtlety

There was once a lovely she-cat who lived in the temple of Venus. This cat fell in love with a mortal man who came there to pray for a wife. She begged the goddess to turn her into a woman so that she could marry him. Meanwhile, the man had also noticed the beauty of the cat, and asked Venus to send him a wife just like the little creature. Venus, despite misgivings, took pity on them both and turned the cat into a girl. The couple were married immediately. But about a month after the wedding they were woken in the night by the scratching of a mouse. To her husband's horror, the woman immediately jumped out of bed, pounced on the mouse, took it in her teeth and killed it. Then she turned on him, with her eyes flashing. Venus appeared, and cautioned the bride: You have changed your form but not your nature – and she changed the girl back to a cat.

Aesop (c. 6th century BC)
Greek fabulist

At last the fox remarks to Puss
"You think yourself a clever beast;
Are you as smart as I? A hundred tricks I know."
"No," says the cat, "I have but one; but that I trow
Is worth a thousand tricks at least."

Jean de la Fontaine (1621–95)
French poet

It is said that the writer's great friend, Madame de la Sablière, on reading this poem got rid of her many beloved dogs and took up with a tribe of black cats instead. French writer Francis Augustus Moncrif asserts that she had a different reason: that one could become too passionately attached to dogs, but with cats one could have a relationship that went no further than one wished.

... she came on a little open patch of green in the middle of which a fine fat Rabbit was sitting. There was no escape ...

"Really," said the Cat, "I don't wish to be troublesome; I wouldn't do it if I could help it; but I am very hungry, I am afraid I must eat you. It is very unpleasant, I assure you, to me as well as to you."

The poor Rabbit begged for mercy.

"Well," said she, "I think it is hard; I do really – and, if the law could be altered, I should be the first to welcome it. But what can a Cat do? You eat the grass; I eat you. But, Rabbit, I wish you would do me a favour."

"Anything to save my life," said the Rabbit.

"It is not exactly that," said the Cat; "but I haven't been used to killing my own food, and it is disagreeable. Couldn't you die?"

James Anthony Froude (1818–94)
English historian and man of letters
from *The Cat's Pilgrimage*, 1870

Once fairly established in her new quarters, the kit lost no time in commencing hostilities against the rats, and blood, not butter-milk, became her war-cry. One day as she sat admiring herself in the glass, a large rat unexpectedly appeared in the kitchen; and although but little larger than himself, Kittie at once gave chase, not only to his hole, but into his hole. For the next three minutes the squeaking was quite harrowing to listen to; but presently pussy re-appeared stern foremost, and dragging with her the rat – dead … In one moment she had bounded from kit to cat-hood. Buttermilk and a looking-glass! Bah! Blood alone could satisfy her ambition now.

Little Muffie was left that night in sole charge of the kitchen, and next morning, no less than five large rats, lay side by side on the hearth, as if waiting a *post mortem*, and wee pussie, with her white breast dabbled in gore, exhausted and asleep, lay beside them. In less than a week, she had bagged upwards of forty.

William Gordon Stables (1840–1910)
Scottish writer
from *Cats, Their Points and Classification*, 1877

Romance

Female cats are very lascivious, and make advances to the male.

Aristotle (384–322 BC)
Greek philsopher

Women condemned to death for adultery are thrown into the Nile,
sewn up in a sack with a female cat. This refinement of cruelty
is perhaps due to the oriental idea that of all female
animals the cat bears the closest resemblance to
womankind, in her suppleness, her slyness,
her coaxing ways, and her inconstancy.

Monsieur Prisse d'Avennes (1807–79)
French Egyptologist

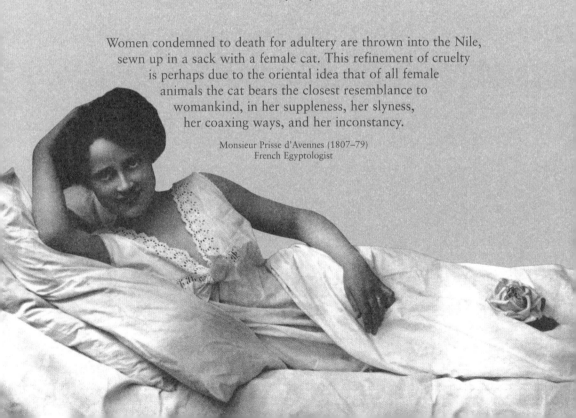

&Sensuality

It is easy to understand
why the rabble dislike cats.
A cat is beautiful; it suggests ideas of luxury,
cleanliness, voluptuous pleasures.

Charles Baudelaire (1821–67)
French poet

"To bring in a cat."

Japanese expression for obtaining the services of a geisha.

... flirting, falling, and yawning anywhere,
Like women who want no contract ...

Louis MacNeice (1907–63)
Irish poet

47

Has it not often occurred to you to wonder why cats, whose modesty leads them to carry on their love-making under the shroud of night and in the solitude of the roof-top, should at the same time sing their amorous duets like impassioned Romeos and perfervid Marguerites, with such piercing shrieks and cries? ... Moncrif describing the assignations of cats on the tiles, proves it as follows: "A mouse came out," he says "and off went our gallant in hot pursuit. The lady, much annoyed as you may suppose, devised an expedient to preserve her from a repetition of the affront: this was to scream loudly from time to time whenever she and her lover were enjoying a tête-à-tête. These cries never failed to frighten away the mouse which never again dared to disturb their meetings ... how happy would women think themselves if this were all that were needed to prevent their lovers ever being indifferent to their society!"

Marius Vachon
19th-century French writer

"I could do a little singing with a living lover ..."

James Anthony Froude (1818–94)
English historian and man of letters
The she-cat's comment from *The Cat's Pilgrimage*, 1870

"Ah, Bébé, he was handsome! And his eyes sparkled with the flame of kindling love. He was the ideal cat of whom we sing when gazing on the moon veiled by city smoke. At last, in a high-pitched rapturous voice, he exclaimed, 'Divine Minette, I adore thee.' I felt my tail expand at his audacity, but my heart expanded in unison, for I already felt that he was mine ...

"If you had only heard his eloquence, Bébé. I confess I felt flattered and puffed up with pride, and saw myself prospectively arrayed in all the finery he promised to lay at my feet; lace, collars, jewels, and a superb ermine muff. This last gift brought me into great trouble.

"I was naturally indolent – he pictured to me a life of ease with its soft carpets, velvet and brocade cushions, arm-chairs, sofas, and all sorts of fine furniture. He assured me that his mistress – an ambassador's wife – would be delighted to receive me whenever I cared to visit her, and that all the collection which made her apartments a magazine of curiosities was at my disposal.

"Oh, it was delightful to dream of being waited on so ...

"He assured me I was simply perfect, in tones so musical, that I heard the old landlady below screaming with delight. I said I felt lonely, and he swore eternal fidelity – Oh! How he did swear – and promised a life of cloudless joy. In a word I was to become his wife, and the ambassador's title cat.

"What more need I add? I followed him and thus became Madame de Brisquet."

from *The Love Adventures of a French Cat*, adapted from the French by J. Thomson,
in *Public and Private Life of Animals*, 1876

In this tale, two sister cats, Bébé (poor and happy) and Minette (rich and heartsore) exchange a correspondence. Minette's honeymoon with the seductive M. de Brisquet lasts only fifteen days and he soon leaves her for an exotic Chinese cat. Minette becomes philosophical, renounces the world and retires to her apartments to ponder the possibility of cats being transformed into women. However, this is not to be, as Minette's fashionable mistress is not pleased with her miserable cat, and orders her to be sewn in a fine linen bag and drowned in the river. At the last minute, both the mistress and her maid are struck unaccountably dead, and Minette returns to live in amiable poverty with her sister Bébé.

From the Persian Snow, at Dr Darwin's,
to Miss Po Felina, at the Palace, Lichfield.

Dear Miss Pussey,

As I sat, the other day, basking myself in the Dean's walk, I saw you, in your stately palace, washing your beautiful round face, and elegantly brindled ears, with your velvet paws, and whisking about, with graceful sinuosity, your meandering tail. That trecherous hedgehog, Cupid, concealed himself behind your tabby beauties, and darting one of his too well aimed quills, pierced, O cruel imp! my fluttering heart.

Ever since that fatal hour have I watched, day and night, in my balcony, hoping that the stillness of the starlight evenings might induce you to take the air on the leads of the palace. Many serenades have I sung under your windows: and, when you failed to appear, with the sound of my voice made the vicarage re-echo through all its winding lanes and dirty alleys. All heard me but my cruel Fair-one; she, wrapped in fur, sat purring with contented insensibility, or slept with untroubled dreams.

Though I cannot boast those delicate varieties of melody with which you sometimes ravish the ear of night, and stay the listening stars; though you sleep hourly on the lap of the favourite of the muses, and are patted by those fingers which hold the pen of science; and every day, with her permission, dip your white whiskers in delicious cream; yet am I not destitute of all advantages of birth, education, and beauty. Derived from Persian kings, my snowy fur yet retains the whiteness and splendour of their ermine ...

You know not, dear Miss Pussey Po, the value of the address you neglect. New milk have I, in flowing abundance, and mice pent up in twenty garrets, for your food and amusement.

Permit me, this afternoon, to lay at your divine feet the head of an enormous Norway Rat, which has even now stained my paws with its gore. If you will do me the honour to sing the following song, which I have taken the liberty to write, as expressing the sentiments I wish you to entertain, I will bring a band of catgut and catcall, to accompany you in chorus ...

Deign, most adorable charmer, to purr your assent to this my request, and believe me to be with the profoundest respect, your true admirer,

Snow

Answer

I am but too sensible of the charms of Mr. Snow, but while I admire the spotless whiteness of his ermine, and the tyger-strength of his commanding form, I sigh in secret, that he, who sucked the milk of benevolence and philosophy, should yet retain the extreme of that fierceness, too justly imputed to the Grimalkin race. Our hereditary violence is perhaps commendable when we exert it against the foes of our protectors, but deserves much blame when it annoys their friends ...

Marry you, Mr. Snow, I am afraid I cannot; since, though the laws of our community might not oppose our connection, yet those of principle, of delicacy, of duty to my mistress, do very powerfully oppose it ...

I am, dear Mr. Snow
Your ever obliged
Po Felina

The English physician and poet Erasmus Darwin (1731–1802) and the poet Anna Seward (1747–1809) exchanged these letters in the name of their cats, Snow and Po Felina.

THE LOVER

Whose mistress feared a mouse, declareth that he
would become a Cat if he might have his desire

If I might alter kind,
      What, think you, I would be?
Nor Fish, nor Fowl, nor Flea, nor Frog,
      Nor Squirrel on the Tree;
The Fish the Hook, the Fowl
      The lymed Twig doth catch,
The Flea the Finger, and the Frog
      The Bustard doth dispatch.
The Squirrel thinking nought,
      That feately cracks the Nut;
The greedy Goshawk wanting prey
      In dread of Death doth put;
But scorning all these kinds,
      I would become a Cat,
To combat with the creeping Mouse,
      And scratch the screeking Rat.

I would be present, aye,
      And at my Lady's call;
To guard her from the fearful Mouse,
      In Parlour and in Hall;
In Kitchen, for his Life,
      He should not show his Head;
The Pear in Poke should lie untoucht
      When she were gone to Bed.
The Mouse should stand in Fear,
      So should the squeaking Rat;
And this would I do if I were
      Converted to a Cat.

George Turberville (1540–1610)
English poet and scholar

How many women have a passion for cats,
and how many men are women in this respect.

Francis Augustus Moncrif (1687–1770)
French poet and writer
from *Lettres Sur Les Chats*, 1727

They are the cleanest, cunningest, and most intelligent
things I know, outside the girl you love, of course.

Mark Twain (1835–1910)
American writer

Most fascinating of musk-cats! But at the same time
as charming as an Angora cat, just the kind that I like.

Heinrich Heine (1797–1856), German poet, to Camille Seldon, 1855.

A Man possessed a Cat on which he doted.
So fine she was, so soft, so silky-coated –
Her very mew had quality!
He was as mad as mad could be.
So one fine day, by dint of supplications,
And tears, and charms, and conjurations,
He worked upon the powers above
To turn her woman; and the loon
Took her to wife that very afternoon.
Before, 'twas fondness crazed him:
now 'twas love!

Jean de la Fontaine (1621–95)
French poet
from "Cat into Lady"
translated by Edward Marsh

Motherhood

I am on terms of recognition with several small streets of cats, about the Obelisk in Saint George's Fields, and also in the vicinity of Clerkenwell-green, and also in the back settlements of Drury-lane. In appearance, they are very like the women among whom they live. They seem to turn out of their unwholesome beds into the street, without any preparation. They leave their young families to stagger about the gutters, unassisted, while they frouzily quarrel and swear and scratch and spit, at street corners. In particular, I remark that when they are about to increase their families (an event of frequent recurrence) the resemblance is strongly expressed in a certain dusty dowdiness, down-at-heel self-neglect, and general giving up of things. I cannot honestly report that I have seen a feline matron of this class washing her face when in an interesting condition.

Charles Dickens (1812–70)
English novelist
from *The Uncommercial Traveller*, 1860

She would come home in a
shocking state, all bedraggled,
her fur so torn and dirty
that she had to spend a whole
week licking herself clean.
After that she would resume
her supercilious airs …
And one fine morning she would
be found with a litter of kittens.

Émile Zola (1840–1902)
French novelist

On April 5th our one daffodil came into flower
& our cat, Charlie Chaplin, had a kitten.

ATHENAEUM   APRIL

Athenaeum is like a prehistoric lizard, in very little. He emerged very strangely – as though hurtling through space – flung by the indignant Lord. I attended the birth. Charles implored me. He behaved so strangely; he became a beautiful tragic figure with blue-green eyes, terrified and wild. He would only lie still when I stroked his belly & said: "it's all right, old chap. Its bound to happen to a man sooner or later." And, in the middle of his pangs, his betrayer, a wretch of a cat with a face like a penny bun & the cat-equivalent of a brown bowler hat, rather rakish over one ear, began to *howl* from outside. Fool that I have been! said Charles, grinding his claws against my sleeve. The second kitten April was born during the night, a sunny compact little girl. When she sucks she looks like a small infant saying its prayers & *knowing* that Jesus loves her. She always has her choice of the strawberry, the chocolate and the pistacchio one; poor little Athenaeum has to put up with an occasional grab at the lemon one ... They are both loves; their paws inside are very soft, very pink, just like unripe raspberries.

Katherine Mansfield (1888–1923), New Zealand-born writer, from a letter to English writer Virginia Woolf, around April 10th, 1919.

Matilda's busy mothering these days.
She's no less regal, and her plumy tail
Waves even more triumphantly, as one
With banners marching.
        She has kinder grown,
Much more approachable and folksy, and
When I approach the basket where she lies
With three adorable fat offspring, formed
In her own august image, save that each
One wears a white shirt-front (which makes me ask
Jocosely: "What price father anyway?")
She graciously permits me to caress
And even lift one catling from the rest.
Confidingly her amber eyes meet mine
As if to say:
      "We women understand ..."

Mazie W. Carruthers
20th-century English poet

The three merriest things
in the world are a cat's kitten,
a goat's kid and a young widow.

Irish proverb

*The Italians believe that the M marking to be seen
on the forehead of tabby cats is the mark of the Madonna.
The tabby cat was said to have been put by her into the
manger to comfort the crying baby Jesus.*

This foolish, striped, grey puss is not a crooning mother;
in this gently purring mother cat is nature herself,
a mother a million times older and more passionate
than my puzzled pussy.

Karel Čapek (1890–1938)
Czech journalist and writer

Thy clutching feet

bepat the ground,

And all their harmless

claws disclose

Like prickles of an early rose,

While softly from

thy whisker'd cheek

Thy half-closed eyes peer,

mild and meek.

Joanna Baillie
(1762–1851)
Scottish playwright and poet

For she,
that will with kittens jest,
Should bear a kitten's joke,

William Cowper (1731–1800)
English poet
translated from the Latin of Vincent Bourne

Familiars of

The characteristics of womankind lend themselves
naturally to the practice of sorcery. Women read
the secrets of the heart more clearly than men ...
the fireside cat, and the implement used for
house-cleaning, are both familiar to old women;
therefore it was that the cat, in company with the
broom, was regarded as the accomplice of sorcery.

Champfleury (Jules-Fleury Husson) (1821–82)
French writer

A cat, with its phosphorescent eyes that stand it in the stead of
lanterns, and sparks flashing from its back, moves fearlessly through
the darkness, where it meets wandering ghosts, witches, alchemists,
necromancers, resurrectionists, lovers, thieves, murderers, grey-coated
patrols, and all the obscure larvae that emerge and work by
night only. It seems to know more than the latest special
from the sabbath, and does not hesitate to rub up against
Mephistopheles' lame leg.

Théophile Gautier (1811–72)
French poet and writer

It is the neighbour's cat that makes one believe there is a hell.

Robert Lynd (1879 –1949)
Irish essayist and critic

Witches

Fontenelle tells us that in his childhood he had been taught to believe that on St. John's Eve never a cat was left in the towns, because on that day they all met for a great general Sabbath.
In most of the ancient provinces of France popular legend has tales of wizard cats. In Brittany, of yore, such cats as had not had the tips of their tails cut off were wont to assemble on a certain date by moonlight, on some deserted heath, not far from the Fairies' Rock and the Standing Stones. There they held council, as grave as priests and judges.

Marius Vachon
19th-century French writer

Never have a black cat in the house because they are
unearthly creatures and things of the devil.
But white cats are good for they are the white ghosts of ladies.

Gypsy superstition

A famous Scotch witch, Isobel Gowdie, burnt in 1662,
actually confessed that she changed to a Cat at night
and roamed the neighbourhood learning secrets.

Charles Platt
from *"Mieaou!" A Treatise on Cats*, 1934

To dream of cats is considered very unlucky. In some of the more unfrequented districts of Scotland, the good folks are still very careful to shut up their cats in the house, on Hallowe'en, i.e., the 31st of October. And they tell me, that those cats that have managed to escape incarceration, that night may be seen, by those brave enough to look, scampering over hill and dell, and across the lonely moors, each one ridden by a brownie, a bogle, a spunkie, or some other infernal jockey, in fact, a devil's own steeplechase. And, they say, those cats never produce young again; or, if they do, the sooner the kittens are put out of sight the better; they are subject to startings in their sleep – no wonder – have a weird unearthly look about their eyes, and soon pine away, and die, and go – we shudder to say whither.

William Gordon Stables (1840–1910)
Scottish writer
from *Cats: Their Points and Classification*, 1877

Names of witches' cats

Tewhit

Jarmara

JESO

Prickear

Peyewacket

Griezl Greedigut

In Caithness, in 1718, William Montgomery insisted that he was haunted by hordes of cats who gathered round his home by night and talked in human voices. One night, tormented beyond endurance, he attacked the beasts and killed two, wounding some others. The next day two old ladies of the village were found dead in their beds and another was found to be badly gashed on the knee, with no explanation.

Requiescat

Yu kant induce one, by enny ordinary means,
to accept ov death, – they actually skorn tew die.

Josh Billings (1818–85)
American humorist
from *Josh Billings, His Works Complete*, 1876

All her pains are over, and that innocent little soul "free'd by the
throbbing impulse we call death", is enjoying itself somewhere else.

Edith Carrington
from *The Cat: Her Place in Society and Treatment*, 1896

ELEGY ON DE MARSAY

Come cats and kittens everywhere,
    What'er of cat the world contains,
From Tabby on the kitchen stair
To Tiger burning in his lair
    Unite your melancholy strains ...

And (when we've adequately moaned),
    For all the world to wonder at,
Let this great sentence be intoned:
No cat so sweet a mistress owned;
    No mistress owned so sweet a cat.

James Kenneth Stephen (1859–92)
English writer and editor

A cat has nine lives,
and a woman has nine cat's lives.

Thomas Fuller (1608–61)
English clergyman

May'st thou on Rats and Mice be fed,
And lose thy Bacon, Cheese, and Bread.
May all thy Goods and Furniture,
If thou has any to secure,
By those vile Vermin be destroyed;
And may thy House be still annoy'd,
And stink so with them, ne'er to be
Kept clean by any Housewifery.
Further, my Curses to compleat,
May'st thou at length be sweetly beat,
With Cat of Nine-Tales, and then swing,
In Hempen or in Cat-gut string.

J. A. Belcher
19th-century English poet
from a poem written to someone who had cut off the ears
of his favourite female cat.